The Holy Book of Revelation

The Final Message of Jesus Christ

by

C. Lincoln Humes

Cork Hill Press
Carmel

CORK HILL PRESS™

Cork Hill Press
597 Industrial Drive, Suite 110
Carmel, IN 46032-4207
1-866-688-BOOK
www.corkhillpress.com

Reorganization of the text of The Book of Revelation and footnotes
by C. Lincoln Humes, Pastor,
Universal Church Of God

Trade Paperback Edition: 1-59408-293-6

Library of Congress Card Catalog Number: 2005920575

Printed in the United States of America

1 3 5 7 9 10 8 6 4 2

For every dark cloud there is a silver lining
and when that hope comes from God above
It creates an abundance of living water.

To my beloved brothers and sisters in Christ and all who choose to read this book to glean a better understanding of the holy things of God and Jesus Christ I give you thanks. Also I pray that you gain the understanding which you seek through the Holy Spirit of God in letting the direction of God be the driving force through which you start, walk and end each day as you pursue life eternal.

How This Work Came About

As I looked in Christendom I saw that our lives were filled with sin, shortcomings and only sporadic hints of the victories promised by our Lord and Savior Jesus Christ. Seeing our failings I prayed for our deficit before going to bed one night and asked The Lord to reveal to me what we as Christians need to straighten our walk before Him. That night, after falling asleep God woke me and directed my mind how to unlock The Book Of Revelation. He showed me the book and told me how difficult it is to read and understand (As He ordained until the end of time). But! He said to me; "I will show you how to make it plain that all truth seekers can understand."

He showed me that man needs to understand His end-time truth, which is locked in this book – The Book Of Revelation. He then gave me the key to unlock this book of mystery. For many days I could not sleep, eat or work as I pursued this task The Lord had set before my hands.

In finishing this work I did not add or take anything away from the original writing. I was shown all that were needed to understand the book and how to reorganize the text to constitute a smooth story flow. I was shown how to move text together of similar subject matter so that a more global understanding of the topic can be harvested. Similarly I was given the key on how to move subject matter according to their timeline giving a better flow to the history.

Not by my will but by His might and power this work was accomplished.

How To Understand This Work

Please read the text as you would any book ignoring the numbers associated. God will richly bless your mind as you read and comprehend. As you live the knowledge revealed, you will be transported figuratively to living on a different plain where wisdom is the guiding force and humility the nature of your character.

Read the work a second time and you will see that different verses have been brought together. By knowing or cross-referencing the old verse markers, in some places one can see sections of different chapters have been imported to make a topic plain. The old references to verses are indicated by the larger numbers at the start or in the middle of a newly constructed sentence or thought.

This work is still driven by the old story flow and chapter markings of the original scholars; who provided the key divisional markers.

Please read the work a third time and take the footnote numbers page by page and if there are Scriptural text to help make a point; please read and also study these passages of Holy Scripture in depth. In so doing you will understand the message our God wants to make clear to all His people that His kingdom be established here on earth real soon.

With much dedication I give to you from the heart of God my labour of love.

Who Am I

I am a dedicated Christian who commenced my walk in 1974. I studied to be and became a Methodist minister a few years later. As I have grown in The Lord I have come to see many practices espoused by Christian churches that are not of God. I have also come to realize there are things given to us by God and Jesus Christ that are not followed. I have long since thrown away the traditions of men and inculcate the instructions of God according to His light for many years. I never start a day without prayer, Bible study and meditation. I fast on a regular basis and I try to live in harmony with all men and nature. I now have a ministry without the confines of denominational or ethnic barriers. This life has given me peace, love and harmony.

My peace I give to you my peace I leave with you not in the quality of man but as from God through Jesus Christ and being bestowed on me. Much love to you.

C. Lincoln Humes, Pastor.

The Holy Book of Revelation

Chapter 1

1 The Revelation of Jesus Christ, 5 and from
Jesus Christ,[1] the faithful witness, the firstborn
of the dead[2], and the ruler of the kings of
the earth[3]. Unto Him that loves us, and loosed
us from our sins by His blood; 6 and He made
us (to be) kings, priests unto His God and
Father; to Him the glory and the dominion
forever and ever. Amen.

---

[1] *Let it be known from here on that this book is not the book of John but of Jesus Christ The Divine. No other person deserves this name; no one should be called a Rabbi or Reverend or even teacher in regards the Scriptures. These names belong only to God and Jesus Christ.*

[2] *This book makes it clear that no one prior or since Jesus Christ was ever resurrected to eternal life. The first to do so was Jesus Christ. Since Jesus Christ no one else has ever been resurrected to that state of existence; not even Mary the mother of Jesus Christ. There are three key passages of Scriptures after the death of Christ that makes this point plain: 1 Thessalonians 4: 13-17, 1 Corinthians 15: 50-55 and John 5: 24-30*

[3] *At this point within the same context we are moved in a time frame after the coronation of the spiritual and resurrected true Christians. It is a future discourse probably even after 'The Great White Throne Judgment'. This is finally supported by the thought that: We, the true believers have been given our crowns'.*

9 I John, both your brother and partaker with
you in tribulation and kingdom and patience
in Jesus Christ, Grace to you and peace, from
Him who is and who was and who is to come;
and from the seven Spirits, which God gave
Him to show unto his servants the things
which must shortly come to pass and He sent
and signified by His angel unto His servant
John[4]; 2 who bares witness of the word of God,
and of the testimony of Jesus Christ, [even]
of all things that he saw while in the isle that
is called Patmos, for the word of God and
the testimony of Jesus. 10 I was in the Spirit
on the Lord's Day[5] 12 And I turned to see
the voice that spoke with me. And having
turned I saw seven golden candlesticks; 13
and in the midst of the candlesticks One like
unto a son of man, clothed with a garment
down to the foot, and girt about at the breasts
with a golden girdle. 14 And His head and

---

[4] *The author of the book is identified as a John but we do not know which John it is in reference to Biblical John's.*

[5] *This statement often confuses many having them believe it is Sunday.But the day referred to here is the weekly Sabbath. This knowledge is gleaned from Jesus' statement in Mark 2:28. This is the only day that Jesus our Lord says that He is supreme over.*

His hair were white as wool, as white as snow; and His eyes were as a flame of fire; 15 and His feet like unto burnished brass, as if it had been refined in a furnace; and His voice as the voice of many waters. 16 And He had in His right hand seven stars and out of His mouth proceeded a sharp two-edged sword and His countenance was as the sun shining in its strength.[6] 17 And when I saw Him, I fell at His feet as one dead. And He laid His right hand upon me, saying; "Fear not; I am the first and the last...." 18 "...and the Living One; and I was dead, and behold, I am alive for evermore, and I have the keys of death[7]

---

[6] *Here we get a description of the resurrected Jesus Christ. Please note the description He bears. He have hair like wool and skin like a Black Man. We have lived hundreds of years under the influence of European culture believing that Jesus was Caucasian. Geography defies that trend of thought but still some continue to accept that lie. N.B. Race does not save anyone nor does cultural affinity. We are engendered to God by knowing and living His truth as amplified by Jesus Christ: John 14: 15-17.*

[7] *Death here is referred to as the second death that will end in hell fire. That fire which is the word Hades is the holding place of Satan and the fallen demons. It will be a prison made up of fire holding for the demons and Satan for eternity not man. A specific fire that can contain evil spirit beings but will end in the total consummation of flesh and blood of fallen humanity.*

and of Hades. 19 Write therefore the things
which you have seen, and the things which
are, and the things which shall come to pass
hereafter; 20 the mystery of the seven[8] stars
which you saw in my right hand, and the
seven golden candlesticks. The seven stars are
the angels of the seven churches and the
seven candlesticks are seven churches. "3.
Blessed[9] is he that reads, and they that hear
the words of the prophesy, and keep the
things that are written therein for the time is
at hand."

4 John to the seven churches that are in Asia
that are before His throne; and I heard be-
hind me a great voice, as of a trumpet 11 say-
ing; "What you see, write in a book and send
to the seven churches unto Ephesus, and
unto Smyrna, and unto Pergamos, and unto
Thyatira, and unto Sardis, and unto Phila-
delphia, and unto Laodicea."

---

[8] *The number seven in relationship to the discourse represent the seven characteristic of the state of the church in the end-time of man's rule of earth.*

[9] *Jesus Christ confers a blessing to those who read, understand and abide by the things written in the book of Revelation; surely also for keeping all His instructions.*

Chapter 2

1 To the angel of the church in Ephesus write
these things said He that holds the seven stars
in His right hand, He that walks in the middle
of the seven golden candlesticks; 2 " I know
your works, and your toil and patience, and
that you cannot not bear evil men, and did
try them that call themselves apostles, and
they are not, and did find them false; 3 and
you have patience and did labour for my
name's sake, and have not grown weary.[10] 4
But I have (this) against you, that you did
leave your first love[11]. 5 Remember therefore

---

[10] *God shows a church that does most things right; including, looking at the fruits of contemporary apostles to see if their actions match up to the teachings of Jesus Christ.*

[11] *Christ goes straight to the point, despite all their great effort He points out they have left their first love or the proof of their first love. Christ told us what that should be in John 14: 15. In the next statement Christ admonishes the church to return to that way of life: A life of loving The Commandments. In continuing, Christ expects true repentance or He expounds a curse: Removing such a church from His presence and finally ending up in Hades(hell). In the next verse He goes on to say to those who overcome their backsliding He will give eternal life.*

from where you have fallen, and repent and do the first works; or else I come to you and will move your candlestick out of its place, except you repent. 6 But this you have, that you hate the works of the Nicolaitans, which I also hate. 7 He that has an ear let him hear what the Spirit says to the churches. To him that overcome, to him will I give to eat of the tree of life, which is in the Paradise of God."

8. And to the angel of the church in Smyrna write These things said the First and the Last, who was dead, and lived 9 " I know your tribulation, and your poverty, and the blasphemy of them that say they are Jews, and they art not, but are a synagogue of Satan.[12] 10 Fear not the things which you art about to suffer: behold, the devil is about to cast some of you

---

[12] *God here is showing the post Jesus church that there are many who claim to be of the same heritage as Him but they are not. This statement has a two-fold meaning. One that Jews who claim to be Jewish have certain characteristics. Jesus taught us what those characteristics are! Loving, kindness, caring, gentle to name a few. Matthew 5: 3-11 and Galatians 5:22 & 23. Two this also apply to Christians who thinking they are Christian but are not. The Scriptures makes this plain Luke 6: 46 and Matthew 7: 21-23. This same passage of Scripture in Revelation supported by Luke and Matthew applies to Jews and Christians alike.*

into prison, that you may be tried; and you
shall have tribulation ten days. Be you faith-
ful unto death, and I will give you the crown
of life. 11 He that have an ear, let him hear
what the Spirit say to the churches. He that
overcome shall not be hurt of the second
death."

12 and to the angel of the church in
Pergamos write these things said He that has
the sharp two-edged sword.
13 "I know where you dwell, where Satan's
throne is; and you hold fast My name, and
did not deny My faith, even in the days of
Antipas my witness, my faithful one, who was
killed among you, where Satan dwell. 14 But
I have a few things against you, because you
have there some that hold the teaching of
Balaam, who taught Balak to cast a stumbling
block before the children of Israel, to eat

We know what God tells His people what to do. Any group or nation that does the opposite is the congregation of Satan. God tells us to love if hate exists, God tells us to leave vengeance to Him, God tells us not to kill some go to war and some even go to war against their own brothers. Those are the congregation of Satan. God tells us to keep the Sabbaths if one denies them; the deniers are a part of the congregation of Satan.

things sacrificed to idols, and to commit for-
nication. 15 So have you also some that hold
the teaching of the Nicolaitans in like man-
ner. 16 Repent therefore; or else I come to
you quickly, and I will make war against them
with the sword of my mouth. 17 He that have
an ear; let him hear what the Spirit say to the
churches. To him that overcome, to him will
I give of the hidden manna, and I will give
him a white stone, and upon the stone a new
name written, which no one knows but he
that receives it."

18 And to the angel of the church in Thyatira
write these things says the Son of God, who
have His eyes like a flame of fire, and His
feet are like unto burnished brass.
19 "I know your works, and your love and
faith and ministry and patience, and that your
last works are more than the first.
20 But I have (this) against you, that you al-
lowed the woman Jezebel, who call herself a
prophetess; and she teach and seduce my
servants to commit fornication, and to eat

things sacrificed to idols[13]. 21 And I gave her
time that she should repent; and she did not
to repent of her fornication. 22 Behold, I
cast her into a bed, and them that commit
adultery with her into great tribulation, ex-
cept they repent of her works[14]. 23 And I will
kill her children with death; and all the
churches shall know that I am He that search
the reins and hearts and I will give unto each
one of you according to your works. 24 But
to you I say, and to the rest that are in Thyatira,
as many as have not this teaching, which know
not the deep things of Satan, as they call
them; I cast upon you no other burden. 25
Nevertheless that which ye have, hold fast till
I come. 26 And he that overcome, and he
that keep my works unto the end, to him will
I give authority over the nations: 27 and he
shall rule them with a rod of iron, as the ves-
sels of the potter are broken to shivers; as I

---

[13] *God is making us aware that there is a false church that teaches things directly opposite to His word. He is giving time to that false church to change so that she and her off springs are not consumed by His wrath.*

[14] *The work of the false church or Jezebel is easily identifiable; see Mark 7: 7-9*

shall rule them with a rod of iron, as the vessels of the potter are broken to shivers; as I
also have received of my Father: 28 and I
will give him the morning star. 29 He that
have an ear, let him hear what the Spirit say
to the churches."

Chapter 3

1. And to the angel of the church in Sardis[15]
write: These things says He that have the
seven Spirits of God, and the seven stars; "I
know your works, that you have a name that
you live and you are dead. 2 Be you watch-
ful, and establish the things that remain,
which were ready to die for I have found no
works of yours perfected before my God. 3
Remember therefore how you have received
and did hear; and keep, and repent. If there-
fore you shall not watch, I will come as a thief,
and you shall not know what hour I will come
upon you.
4 But you have a few names in Sardis that did
not defile their garments and they shall walk
with me in white; for they are worthy. 5 He
that overcome shall be arrayed in white gar-

---

[15] *The Church group that holds this character feels superior to others but still does not measure up to the teachings of Jesus Christ. Still some in that system holds on to the teachings of God but have some shortcomings.*

ments; and I will in no wise blot his name out
of the book of life, and I will confess his name
before My Father, and before His angels. 6
He that have an ear, let him hear what the
Spirit says to the churches."

7 And to the angel of the church in Philadel-
phia write these things says He that is holy,
He that is true, He that have the key of David,
He that open and none shall shut, and that
shuts and none open. 8 I know your works
(behold, I have set before you a door opened,
which none can shut), that you have a little
power, and did keep My Word, and did not
deny My name. 9 Behold, I give of the syna-
gogue of Satan, of them that say they are Jews,
and they are not, but do lie; behold, I will
make them to come and worship before your
feet, and to know that I have loved you. 10
Because you did keep the word of My pa-
tience, I also will keep you from the hour of
trial, that which is to come upon the whole
world, to try them that dwell upon the earth.
11 I come quickly hold fast that which you
have, that no one take your crown. 12 He
that overcome, I will make him a pillar in the
temple of My God, and he shall go out no

more: and I will write upon him the name of
My God, and the name of the city of My God,
the new Jerusalem, which comes down out
of heaven from My God, and mine own new
name. 13 He that has an ear, let him hear
what the Spirit says to the churches." [16]

14 And to the angel of the church in Laodicea
write: These things said The Amen, The
Faithful and True Witness, The Beginning
of the creation of God 15 "I know your works,
that you are neither cold nor hot; I would
you were cold or hot. 16 So because you are
lukewarm, and neither hot nor cold, I will
spew you out of My mouth. 17 Because you
say, I am rich, and have gotten riches, and
have need of nothing; and knows not that
you art the wretched one and miserable and
poor and blind and naked 18 I counsel you
to buy of Me gold refined by fire, that you
may become rich; and white garments, that
you may

---

[16] *There is a group present in the final age that adheres to the teachings of God, that keeps His word despite the false churches saying that we do not need to be keeping The Word of God. That group will over come all the false accusiations.*

clothe yourself, and the shame of your nakedness be not made manifest; and eye salve to anoint your eyes that you may see[17]. 19 As
many as I love, I reprove and chasten be zealous therefore, and repent. 20 Behold, I stand
at the door and knock if any man hears my voice and open the door, I will come in to him, and will sup with him, and he with Me.
21 He that overcome, I will give to him to sit down with me in my throne, as I also overcame, and sat down with my Father in His
throne. 22 He that has an ear, let him hear what the Spirit says to the churches."

---

[17] *God is calling all truth seekers to clean their lenses as if wearing glasses that they might perceive His truth. Evident from Matthew 15:14 one must know God before one attempts to teach His ways.*

Chapter 4

1 After these things I saw, and behold, a door
opened in heaven, and the first voice that I
heard, (a voice) as of a trumpet speaking with
me, one saying, come up here, and I will show
you the things which must come to pass here-
after. 2 Straightway I was in the Spirit and
behold, there was a throne set in heaven, and
one sitting upon the throne; 3 and He that
sat (was) to look upon like a jasper stone and
a sardius and a rainbow round about the
throne, like an emerald to look upon.
4 And round about the throne (were) four
and twenty thrones and upon the thrones
four and twenty elders sitting, arrayed in
white garments; and on their heads crowns
of gold. 5 And out of the throne proceed
lightenings, thunderings and voices. And
seven lamps of fire burning before the
throne, which are the seven Spirits of God; 6
and before the throne, as it were a sea of glass
like a crystal; and in the middle of the throne,
and round about the throne, four living crea-
tures full of eyes before and behind. 7 And
the first creature like a lion, and the second

creature like a calf, and the third creature had a face as of a man, and the fourth creature like a flying eagle. 8 and the four living creatures, having each one of them six wings, are full of eyes round about and within[18] and they have no rest day and night, Saying; "Holy, holy, holy, (is) The Lord God, The Almighty, who was and who is and who is to come." 9 And when the living creatures shall give glory and honor and thanks to Him that sits on the throne, to Him that lives for ever and ever, 10 the four and twenty elders fall down before Him that sits on the throne, and worship Him that live forever and ever, and cast their crowns before the throne, Saying; 11 "Worthy are You, our Lord and our God, to receive the glory and the honor and the power for You did create all things, and because of Your will they exist, and were created."[19]

---

[18] *We are given a glimpse into the throne room of God. In the seat of the Most Holy of Holies we see the creatures that is similar to the creatures that The prophet Ezekiel saw; Ezekiel 1: 4-14.*

[19] *The four creatures gave thanks to Jesus Christ through whom all things were created. This piece of Scripture parallel that of John 1:1-3*

Chapter 5

1 And I saw in the right hand of Him that sat
on the throne a book written within and on
the back, sealed with seven seals. 2 And I saw
a strong angel proclaiming with a great voice,
"Who is worthy to open the book, and to loose
the seals?" 3 And no one in the heaven, or
on the earth, or under the earth, was able to
open the book, or to look thereon.
4 And I wept much, because no one was
found worthy to open the book, or to look
thereon 5 and one of the elders said to me;
"Weep not; behold, the Lion that is of the
tribe of Judah, The Root of David[20], have over-
come to open the book and the seven seals."

6 And I saw in the middle of the throne and
of the four living creatures, and in the midst

---

[20] *Here we know that the pronouncement is that Jesus Christ is the one capable of reading the book, Isaiah 11:1,2&10.*

of the elders, a Lamb[21] standing, as though it
had been slain, having seven horns, and seven
eyes, which are the seven Spirits of God, sent
out into all the earth. 7 And he came, and he
took (it) out of the right hand of Him that
sat on the throne. 8 And when He had taken
the book, the four living creatures and the
twenty-four elders fell down before The
Lamb, having each one a harp, and golden
bowls full of incense, which are the prayers
of the saints.
9 And they sing a new song, saying:

> "Worthy are You to take the book,
> and to open the seals thereof
> for you were slain,
> and did purchase unto God
> with Your blood (men) of every tribe,
> and tongue, and people, and nation,
> 10 and made them
> unto our God a kingdom and priests;
> and they shall reign upon earth."

---

[21] *That Lamb is Jesus Christ, slain from the foundation of the world to pay the price for our sins, Revelation 13:8, John 1:29, and 1Peter 1:19 & 20 and Hebrews 9:11-14.*

11 And I saw, and I heard a voice of many
angels round about the throne and the liv-
ing creatures and the elders; and the num-
ber of them was ten thousand times ten thou-
sand, and thousands of thousands[22]; 12 say-
ing with a great voice.

> "Worthy is The Lamb that have been slain
> to receive the power,
> and riches, and wisdom, and might and honor,
> and glory, and blessing.

13 And every created thing which is in the
heaven, and on the earth, and under the
earth, and on the sea, and all things are in
them heard I saying,

> "...Unto Him that sits on the throne,
> and unto The Lamb, (be) the blessing,
> and the honor, and the glory,
> and the dominion, forever and ever."

14 And the four living creatures said; "Amen."
And the elders fell down and worshipped.

---

[22] *Because of the numerical data when we tie verses 10 and 11 we see that the reader is taken into the distant future kingdom of God. Still John will come back to the near future.*

Chapter 6

The First Seal

1. And I saw when the Lamb opened one of
the seven seals, and
I heard one of the four living creatures say-
ing as with a voice of thunder, "Come."
2 And I saw, and behold, a white horse[23], and

[23] *The first seal reveals the first horse (the white horse) and its rider. If one does not read carefully they might think that this is Christ. It is not! Christ does not set out to conquer He wins us by His love. Christ's weapon is a sword this personage have a bow. It speaks to purity in the form of whiteness but it is not Christ in fact it symbolizes false religion. We can be assured that this false Christ has already rode. He has conquered most of the churches of the world. The Church that Jesus left behind and that existed throughout the first four hundred years after He left no way resembles the false mass of what is called Christianity today. The churches which should be Christ-like has been conquered and are being conquered. The Christian churches today live a life of false teachings and practices showing that they have been conquered by the white horse's rider. This conquest started with what Constantine in the fourth century did to the church of God. He outlawed the real teachings of Jesus Christ and His practices as an example for us: the keeping of unchanged Sabbaths and a commandment of loving each other. Now we have what sprang from his change has given rise to the false church and predominantly other churches sprang from that false base making most of the Christian churches of today false but for a very small minority.*

he that sat thereon had a bow; and there was given unto him a crown and he came forth conquering, and to conquer.

The Second Seal

3. And when He opened the second seal, I heard the second living creature saying, "Come." 4 And another [horse] came forth a red horse[24] and to him that sat thereon it was given to take peace from the earth, and that they should slay one another and there was given unto him a great sword.

The Third Seal

5 And when He opened the third seal, I heard the third living creature saying, "Come." And

---

[24] *The red horse and its rider symbolizes the blood of the many who have been and will continue to be shed because the love of many others has gone cold. Jesus came to teach us to love one another, John 15:12. He tried to teach the world that the only way God will recognize us as His; if we love each other. That love have disappeared and humanity have become callous, cruel, uncaring and we shed blood. What we have seen of the blood letting is only a small sampling; it will get progressively worst. See Matthew 24.*

I saw, and behold, a black horse[25]; and he
that sat thereon had a balance in his hand. 6
And I heard as it was a voice in the middle of
the four living creatures saying, "A measure
of wheat for a shilling, and three measures
of barley for a shilling; and the oil and the
wine hurt you not."

The fourth Seal

7 And when He opened the fourth seal, I
heard the voice of the fourth living creature
saying, "Come." 8 And I saw, and behold, a
pale horse and he that sat upon him, his
name was Death; and Hades followed with
him. And there was given unto them authority over the fourth part of the earth, to kill with sword, and with famine, and with death, and by the wild beasts of the earth.

---

[25] *This horse and it's rider symbolizes evil and hate, because humanity will be so prone to selfishness. This state of mind is giving rise to wanton hatred and the killing of each other. The pale horse and rider symbolizes diseases. We are aware that hundreds per day are dying from diseases. It will only get worse sorry to say. The stage is set for SARS and chicken flu and the unexplainable flesh eating bacteria. Are we going to let God's return find us asleep or are we going to get on His road to spiritual recovery?*

The Fifth Seal

9 And when He opened the fifth seal, I saw
underneath the altar[26] the souls of them that
had been slain for the word of God, and for
the testimony which they held 10 and they
cried with a great voice, saying, "How long,
O Master, the Holy and True, do You not
judge and avenge our blood on them that
dwell on the earth?" 11 And there was given
them to each one a white robe; and it was
said unto them, that they should rest yet for
a little time, until their fellow-servants also
and their brethren, who should be killed even
as they were, should have fulfilled (their
course).[27]

---

[26] *John was transported into the Holy of Holies before the altar of God. Through the miracle of perception he became aware of the martyrs of the faith. We know from other accounts that they are in the grave and we also know that God sees and knows everything that goes on here on earth. So we must postulate that John was allowed to see the martyred souls through the optics God uses to perceive things here on earth. Secondarily a bit more difficult to understand is how the blood of those who were martyred for the faith cries to God. The dead in the faith was allowed to come alive and talk through prayer to God from the grave, John witnessed this. God blessed them with a portion of their reward and it comforted them and He placed them back into the sleep of death.*

[27] *More faithful servants of God will be killed for their faith. As common as Christianity is today and with most governments acknowledging the existence of a God this is hard to fathom. But! There will come*

The Sixth Seal

12 And I saw when He opened the sixth seal,
and there was a great earthquake; and the
sun became black as sackcloth of hair, and
the whole moon became as blood; 13 and
the stars of the heaven fell unto the earth, as
a fig tree cast her unripe figs when she is
shaken of a great wind. 14 And the heaven
was removed as a scroll when it is rolled up;
and every mountain and islands were moved
out of their places.[28] 15 And the kings of the
earth, and the princes, and the chief captains,
and the rich, and the strong, and every bond-
man and freeman, hid themselves in the caves
and in the rocks of the mountains; 16 and
they say to the mountains and to the rocks,

---

a time in the future in which more will die for their faith. So we will see a change coming in this world that will create a landscape where true Christianity will be hated again.

[28] *The Holy Scripture is prophesying here that there will be a catastrophic event in the form of an earthquake that will change the face of the earth as we know it today. It will be so strong that the celestial bodies will be obscured by this event. The smoke that rises will finally blot them out. It is fairly easy to see how this can happen because from geological facts we know that the earth can shift on it axis if this occurs it can change the magnetic poles having a great effect on the geology of the earth. If this happens this could bring disasters of great proportions.*

"Fall on us, and hide us from the face of Him
that sit on the throne, and from the wrath of
The Lamb 17 for the great day of their wrath
is come; and who is able to stand?"[29]

---

[29] *The rich and powerful, heads of government who have little time for the true God will be the first to recognize that God lives at this junction of history. Still Christ will not return just yet. Jesus said in Matthew 24: 8 it is only the beginning of sorrows.*

Chapter 8

The Seventh Seal

1 And when He opened the seventh seal,
there followed a silence in heaven about the
space of half an hour. 2 And I saw the seven
angels that stand before God; and there were
given unto them seven trumpets. 3 And an-
other angel came and stood over the altar,
having a golden censer; and there was given
unto him much incense, that he should add
it unto the prayers of all the saints upon the
golden altar which was before the throne.
4 And the smoke of the incense, with the
prayers of the saints, went up before God out
of the angel's hand. 5 And the angel took
the censer; and he filled it with the fire of the
altar, and cast it upon the earth and there
followed thunders, and voices, and
lightenings, and an earthquake.

6 And the seven angels that had the seven trumpets prepared themselves to sound. [30]

The First Trumpet

7. And the first sounded, and there followed hail and fire, mingled with blood, and they were cast upon the earth and the third part of the earth was burnt up, and the third part of the trees was burnt up, and all green grass was burnt up.

The Second Trumpet

8 And the second angel sounded, and as it were a great mountain burning with fire was cast into the sea and the third part of the sea
became blood 9 and there died the third part
of the creatures which were in the sea, [even] they that had life; and the third part of the ships was destroyed.

---

[30] *At the end of the final seal there is attached more disasters that must befall man before things come to a final conclusion. God is probably sifting out the faithful from the weak Christians to see who will stand. This time will definitely be a warning to the entire earth to understand that all man have established cannot stand before His awesome power. Remember that man's government would have become a semblance of peace at this time.*

The Third Trumpet

10 And the third angel sounded, and there
fell from heaven a great star, burning as a
torch, and it fell upon the third part of the
rivers, and upon the fountains of the waters;
11 and the name of the star is called Wormwood
and the third part of the waters became
wormwood; and many men died of the waters,
because they were made bitter.

The Fourth Trumpet

12 And the fourth angel sounded, and the
third part of the sun was smitten, and the
third part of the moon, and the third part of
the stars; that the third part of them should
be darkened, and the day should not shine
for the third part of it, and the night in like
manner.
13 And I saw, and I heard an eagle flying in
mid heaven saying with a great voice;
"Woe, woe, woe, for them that dwell on the
earth, by reason of the other voices of the
trumpet of the three angels, who are yet to
sound."

Chapter 9

The Fifth Trumpet - The First Woe
1. And the fifth angel sounded, and I saw a
star from heaven fallen unto the earth and
there was given to him the key of the pit of
the abyss. 2 And he opened the pit of the
abyss; and there went up a smoke out of the
pit, as the smoke of a great furnace; and the
sun and the air were darkened by reason of
the smoke of the pit. 3 And out of the smoke
came forth locusts upon the earth; and power
was given them, as the scorpions of the earth
has power. 4 And it was said unto them that
they should not hurt the grass of the earth,
neither any green thing, neither any tree, but
only such men as have not the seal of God
on their foreheads. 5 And it was given them
that they should not kill them, but that they
should be tormented five months and their
torment was as the torment of a scorpion,
when it strikes a man.
6 And in those days men shall seek death,
and shall in no wise find it; and they shall
desire to die, and death flee from them. 7

And the shapes of the locusts were like unto horses prepared for war; and upon their heads as it were crowns like unto gold, and their faces were as men's faces.
8 And they
had hair as the hair of women, and their teeth were as of lions.
9 And they had breastplates,
as it were breastplates of iron; and the sound of their wings was as the sound of chariots, of many horses rushing to war.
10 And they have
tails like unto scorpions, and stings; and in their tails is their power to hurt men five months.
11 They have over them as king the angel of the abyss his name in Hebrew is Abaddon, and in the Greek he have the name Apollyon.[31]
12 The first **Woe** is past behold, there come yet two **Woes** hereafter.

The Sixth Trumpet - The Second Woe

13. And the sixth angel sounded, and I heard a voice from the horns of the golden altar which is before God,
14 one saying to the
sixth angel that had one trumpet;

[31] *God allows unholy men to be tortured by weapons of destruction. The torture, administered by creatures not of manmade origins but their acts were so painful that many wanted to die from its torture.*

"Loose the four angels that are bound at the
great river Euphrates."
15 And the four angels were loosed, that had
been prepared for the hour and day and
month and year, that they should kill the third
part of men. 16 And the number of the
armies of the horsemen was twice ten thou-
sand times ten thousand two hundred thou-
sand I heard the number of them.[32]
17 And thus I saw the horses in the vision,
and them that sat on them, having breast-
plates of fire and of hyacinth and of brim-
stone and the heads of lions; and out of their
mouths proceed fire and smoke and brim-
stone. 18 By these three plagues was the third
part of men killed, by the fire and the smoke
and the brimstone, which proceeded out of
their mouths.
19 For the power of the horses is in their
mouth, and in their tails for their tails are
like unto serpents, and have heads; and with
them they hurt. 20 And the rest of mankind,
who were not killed with these plagues, re-

---

[32] *Men of the world even though warring and warmongers are being restrained by four angelic forces. God will eventually release these angels so men are not restrained anymore and their true nature will emerge.*

pented not of the works of their hands, that
they should not worship demons, and the
idols of gold, and of silver, and of brass, and
of stone, and of wood; which can neither see,
nor hear, nor walk 21 and they repented
not of their murders, nor of their sorceries,
nor of their fornication, nor of their thefts.

Chapter 10

The Little Book
1 And I saw another strong angel coming
down out of heaven, arrayed with a cloud;
and the rainbow was upon his head, and his
face was as the sun, and his feet as pillars of
fire; 2 and he had in his hand a little book
open and he set his right foot upon the sea,
and his left upon the earth; 3 and he cried
with a great voice, as a lion roars and when
he cried, the seven thunders uttered their
voices. 4 And when the seven thunders ut-
tered (their voices), I was about to write and
I heard a voice from heaven saying, "Seal up
the things which the seven thunders uttered,
and write them not."
5 And the angel that I saw standing upon the
sea and upon the earth lifted up his right
hand to heaven, 6 and swore by Him that
lives forever and ever, who created the heaven
and the things that are therein, and the earth
and the things that are therein, and the sea
and the things that are therein, that there
shall be delay no longer 7 but in the days of

the voice of the seventh angel, when he is
about to sound, then is finished the mystery
of God, according to the good tidings which
he declared to his servants the prophets.
8 And the voice, which I heard from heaven,
again speaking with me, and saying; "Go, take
the book which is open in the hand of the
angel that stands upon the sea and upon the
earth."

9 And I went unto the angel, saying unto him
that he should give me the little book. And
he said unto me, "Take it, and eat it up and it
shall make your belly bitter, but in thy mouth
it shall be sweet as honey." 10 And I took the
little book out of the angel's hand, and ate it
up and it was in my mouth sweet as honey
and when I had eaten it, my belly was made
bitter.
11 And they say unto me;
"Thou must prophesy again over many
peoples and nations and tongues and kings."

Chapter 11

The Two Witnesses

3 And I will give unto my two witnesses, and
they shall prophesy a thousand two hundred
and threescore days, clothed in sackcloth. 4
These are the two olive trees and the two
candlesticks, standing before the Lord of the
earth. 5 And if any man desires to hurt them,
fire proceed out of their mouths and devour
their enemies; and if any man shall desire to
hurt them, in this manner must he be killed.
6 These have the power to shut the heaven,
that it rain not during the days of their proph-
ecy and they have power over the waters to
turn them into blood, and to smite the earth
with every plague, as often as they shall de-
sire. 7 And when they shall have finished their
testimony, the beast that comes up out of the
abyss shall make war with them, and over-
come them, and kill them. 8 And their dead
bodies (lie) in the street of the great city,
which spiritually is called Sodom and Egypt,
where also their Lord was crucified. 9 And
from among the peoples and tribes and

tongues and nations do look upon their dead
bodies three days and a half, and suffer not
their dead bodies to be laid in a tomb.
10 And they that dwell on the earth rejoice
over them, and make merry; and they shall
send gifts one to another; because these two
prophets tormented them that dwell on the
earth. 11 And after the three days and a half
the breath of life from God entered into
them, and they stood upon their feet; and
great fear fell upon them that beheld them.
12 And they heard a great voice from heaven
saying unto them; "Come up hither." And
they went up into heaven in the cloud; and
their enemies beheld them. 13 And in that
hour there was a great earthquake, and the
tenth part of the city fell; and there were killed
in the earthquake seven thousand persons
and the rest were afraid, and gave glory to
the God of heaven. 14 The second Woe is
past behold, the third Woe comes quickly.

The Seventh Trumpet - The Final Woe (Third)

15 And the seventh angel sounded; and there
followed great voices in heaven, and they said;

"The kingdom of the world is become (the
kingdom) of our Lord, and of His Christ and
He shall reign forever and ever."
16 And the four and twenty elders, who sit
before God on their thrones, fell upon their
faces and worshipped God, 17 saying;
"We give thee thanks, O Lord God, The Al-
mighty, who are and who was because You
have taken Your great power, and did reign.
18 And the nations were angry, and Your
wrath came, and the time of the dead to be
judged, and [the time] to give their reward
to Your servants the prophets, and to the
saints, and to them that fear Your name, the
small and the great and to destroy them that
destroy the earth."
19 And there was opened the temple of God
that is in heaven; and there was seen in His
temple the ark of His covenant; and there
followed lightenings, and voices, and thun-
ders, and an earthquake, and great hail.

Chapter 12

The Great Events - Birth of The True Church
1 And a great sign was seen in heaven a
woman arrayed with the sun, and the moon
under her feet, and upon her head a crown
of twelve stars 2 and she was with child; and
she cried out, travailing in birth, and in pain
to be delivered.[33] 3 And there was seen an-
other sign in heaven and behold, a great red
dragon, having seven heads and ten horns,
and upon his heads seven Diadems.7 And
there was war[34] in heaven Michael and his
angels (going forth) to war with the dragon
and the dragon warred and his angels; 8 And
they prevailed not, neither was their place

---

[33] *The true church of God is being made ready. This piece of Scripture shows that the prophetic dream of Joseph in spiritual symbolism has come true, read Genesis 37: 9. God will have a church based on the character of the twelve tribes of Israel.*

[34] *This event seem to be a flashback in time depicting a time before man, when Satan and his demons warred against the host of God and he took a third of the angels with him as they were cast to earth because of their rebellion.*

found any more in heaven. 9 And the great
dragon was cast down, the old serpent, he
that is called the Devil and Satan, the deceiver
of the whole world; he was cast down to the
earth, and his angels were cast down with him.
4 And his tail drew a third part of the stars of
heaven, and did cast them to the earth and
the dragon stood before the woman that was
about to be delivered, that when she is deliv-
ered he may devour her Child.[35] 5 And she
was delivered of a son, a man child, who is to
rule all the nations with a rod of iron and
her child was caught up unto God, and unto
his throne. 6 And the woman fled into the
wilderness, where she had a place prepared
of God, that there they may nourish her a
thousand two hundred and threescore days.

Satan Looses His Place As The Accuser

10 And I heard a great voice in heaven, saying;
"Now is come the salvation, and the power,
and the kingdom of our God, and the au-
thority of His Christ for the accuser of our

---

[35] *Time move forward to the period just prior to Jesus' birth and Satan's attempt to destroy Mary. Even prior to her he planned and attempted the destruction of the lineage through which He would be conceived.*

brethren is cast down, who accuse them be-
fore our God day and night. 11 And they
overcame him because of the blood of the
Lamb, and because of the word of their testimony; and they loved not their life even unto death.

Satan Attempts To Destroy The Church Of God

12. Therefore rejoice, O heavens, and you that dwell in them. Woe for the earth and for the sea because the devil is gone down unto you, having great angry, knowing that he have but a short time."

13 And when the dragon saw that he was cast down to the earth, he persecuted the woman
that brought forth the man [child]. 14 And
there were given to the woman the two wings of the great eagle, that she might fly into the wilderness unto her place, where she is nourished for a time, and times, and half a time,
from the face of the serpent. 15 And the
serpent cast out of his mouth after the woman water as a river, that he might cause her to be
carried away by the stream. 16 And the earth
helped the woman, and the earth opened

her mouth[36] and swallowed up the river
which the dragon cast out of his mouth. 17
And the dragon waxed angry with the
woman, and went away to make war with the
rest of her seed, that keep the command-
ments of God[37], and hold the testimony of
Jesus.

---

[36] *As the lineage of Jesus was about to cross the Red Sea Satan made a bold stand to destroy the people of God but the Red Sea was gracious to them. Moses and all the freed slaves crossed on dry land. Exodus 14: 1-29*

[37] *Satan in the final age of man sets his sight on the true believers; those who have the faith of Jesus and keeps the commandments of God.*

Chapter 14

The Elect With Christ - 144 Thousand

1 And I saw, and behold, the Lamb standing on the Mount Zion, and with Him a hundred and forty and four thousand[38], having His Name, and the name of His Father, written on their foreheads. 2 And I heard a voice from heaven, as the voice of many waters, and as the voice of a great thunder and the voice which I heard as of harpers harping with their harps 3 and they sing as it were a new song before the throne, and before the four living creatures and the elders and no man could learn the song save the hundred and forty and four thousand, they that had been purchased out of the earth. 4 These are they that were not defiled with women; for they

---

[38] *Jesus Christ will be selecting 144 thousand to start His kingdom, these will comprise prophets, holy men of old, apostles, martyred saints and those who died in the faith. Some will be selected from those living while His return is taking place. John 5: 24-30, 1 Thessalonians 4: 13-18 and 1 Corinthians 15: 20-23.*

are virgins[39]. These (are) they that follow the
Lamb wherever He goes. These were pur-
chased from among men, the first fruits unto
God and unto The Lamb. 5 And in their
mouth was found no lie they are without
blemish.
6 And I saw another angel flying in mid
heaven, having eternal good tidings to pro-
claim unto them that dwell on the earth, and
unto every nation and tribe and tongue and
people; 7 and he said with a great voice;
"Fear God, and give Him glory; for the hour
of His judgment is come and worship Him
that made the heaven and the earth and sea
and fountains of waters."

The Commandment Keepers - The Elect

12 Here is the patience of the saints, they that
keep the commandments of God, and the
faith of Jesus[40]. 13 And I heard the voice from

---

[39] *These true believers that follow Jesus Christ numbered among the 144 thousand never practiced false religion.*

[40] *To qualify the righteous must have the faith of Jesus Christ and have kept the commandments. It is a dreadful pity so many Christians believe that the commandments are no longer necessary. If they had listened to Jesus and studied His action they would have learned differently. i.e. Matthew 5:15-19, John 14: 15-17 and Mark 7: 7-9.*

heaven saying;
"Write, blessed are the dead who die in the
Lord from henceforth yea, says the Spirit, that
they may rest from their labors; for their
Works follow with them."
14 And I saw, and behold, a white cloud; and
on the cloud (I saw) one sitting like unto a
son of man, having on his head a golden
crown, and in his hand sharp sickle. 15 And
another angel came out from the temple,
crying with a great voice to him that sat on
the cloud;
"Send forth thy sickle, and reap for the hour
to reap is come; for the harvest of the earth
is ripe." 16 And he that sat on the cloud cast
his sickle upon the earth; and the earth was
reaped.*

---

* *God gathers His saints according to His standards from among men. This 144 thousand will be the core of government of God led by Jesus Christ.*

Chapter 13

The False System - Tool Of Satan/The Dragon

1. And he stood upon the sand of the sea.
And I saw a beast coming up out of the sea,
having ten horns, and seven heads, and on
his horns ten diadems, and upon his heads
names of blasphemy.
2 And the beast, which I saw, was like unto a
leopard, and his feet were as of a bear, and
his mouth as the mouth of a lion and the
dragon gave him his power, and his throne,
and great authority.
3 And one of his heads as though it had been
smitten unto death; and his death-stroke was
healed and the whole earth wondered after
the beast; 4 and they worshipped the dragon,
because he gave his authority unto the beast;
and they worshipped the beast, saying, who
is like unto the beast? And who is able to war
with Him? 5 and there was given to him a
mouth speaking great things and blasphe-
mies; and there was given to him authority
to continue forty and two months.

6 And he opened his mouth for blasphemies
against God, to blaspheme His name, and
His tabernacle, them that dwell in the heaven.
7 And it was given unto him to make war with
the saints, and to overcome them and there
was given to him authority over every tribe
and people and tongue and nation. 8 And
all that dwell on the earth shall worship him,
whose name hath not been written from the
foundation of the world in the book of life of
The Lamb that hath been slain.

16: 13 And I saw out of the mouth of the
dragon, and out of the mouth of the beast,
and out of the mouth of the false prophet,
three unclean spirits, as it were frogs: 14 for
they are spirits of demons, working signs;
which go forth unto the kings of the whole
world, to gather them together unto the war
of the great day of God, the Almighty[41]. 15
(Behold, I come as a thief. Blessed is he that
watches, and keeps his garments, lest he
walked naked, and they see his shame.) 16

---

[41] *Satan will use his powers in a last offensive to utilize sinful man to go up against God.*

And they gathered them together into the
place which is called in Hebrew Har-
magedon. 9 If any man have an ear, let him
hear.

10 If any man [is] for captivity, into captivity
he goes if any man shall kill with the sword,
with the sword must he be killed. Here is the
patience and the faith of the saints. 11 And I
saw another beast coming up out of the earth;
and he had two horns like unto lamb, and
he spoke as a dragon[42]. 12 And he exercise
all the authority of the first beast in his sight.
And he make the earth and them dwell
therein to worship the first beast, whose
death-stroke was healed. 13 And he did great
signs, that he should even make fire to come
down out of heaven upon the earth in the
sight of men.
14 And he deceive them that dwell on the
earth by reason of the signs which it was given
him to do in the sight of the beast; saying to

---

[42] *A second beast power will rise to rule man and separate them farther from God. He will copy closely the markings of God but instead of the forehead it will be in the hand. Some will have his same false mark in their foreheads like true believers. However the mark of the false beast will affect ones ability to participate in the world's commerce.*

them that dwell on the earth, that they should make an image to the beast who have the stroke of the sword and lived. 15 And it was given (unto him) to give breath to it, to the image to the breast, that the image of the beast should both speak, and cause that as many as should not worship the image of the beast should be killed. 16 And he cause all, the small and the great, and the rich and the poor, and the free and the bond, that there be given them a mark on their right hand, or upon their forehead 17 and that no man should be able to buy or to sell, save he that have the mark, the name of the beast or the number of his name. 18 Here is wisdom. He that have understanding, let him count the number of the beast; for it is the number of a man and his number is Six hundred and sixty and six[43].

14:17 Another angel came out from the temple which is in heaven, he also having a sharp sickle. 18 And another angel came out from the altar, he that have power over fire;

---

[43] *The final beast power will have the number 666 which will be easily identifiable as that of an ordinary man.*

and he called with a great voice to him that
had the sharp sickle, saying;
"Send forth your sharp sickle, and gather the
clusters of the vine of the earth; for her grapes
are fully ripe"
19 And the angel cast his sickle into the earth,
and gathered the vintage of the earth, and
cast it into the winepress, the great, of the
wrath of God. 20 And the winepress are trod-
den without the city, and there came out
blood from the winepress, even unto the
bridles of the horses, as far as a thousand and
six hundred furlongs.

15

1 And I saw another sign in heaven, great
and marvelous, seven angels having seven
plagues[44], [which are] the last, for in them is
finished the wrath of God.

5 And after these things I saw, and the temple
of the tabernacle of the testimony in heaven
was opened 6 and there came out from the
temple the seven angels that had the seven

---

[44] *Like with the Egyptians in the exodus God will use plagues seven to be exact, to see if He can bring man to His way of thinking and acting.*

plagues, arrayed with [precious] stone, pure[and] bright, and girt about their breasts with golden girdles.

7 And one of the four living creatures gave unto the seven angels seven golden bowls full of the wrath of God, who lives forever and
ever. 8 And the temple was filled with smoke from the glory of God, and from His power; and none was able to enter into the temple, till the seven plagues of the seven angels should be finished.

16

1 And I heard a great voice out of the temple, saying to the seven angels,
"Go you, and pour out the seven bowls of the wrath of God into the earth."

2 And the first went, and poured out his bowl into the earth; and it became a noisome and grievous sore upon the men that had the mark of the beast, and that worshipped his image.

3 And the second poured out his bowl into
the sea; and it became blood as of a dead
man; and every living soul died, [even] the
things that were in the sea.

4 And the third poured out his bowl into the
rivers and the fountains of the waters; and it
became blood. 5 And I heard the angel of
the waters saying,
"Righteous are You, who are and who was,
You Holy One, because You did Your judge-
ment 6 for they poured out the blood of the
saints and the prophets, and blood has You
given them to drink they are worthy."

7 And I heard another from the altar saying,
"Yea, O Lord God, The Almighty, true and
righteous are Your judgments"

8 And the fourth poured out his bowl upon
the sun; and it was given unto it to scorch
men with fire. 9 And men were scorched
with great heat and they blasphemed the
name of God who have the power over these
plagues; and they repented not to give Him
glory.

10 And the fifth poured out his bowl upon the throne of the beast; and his kingdom was darkened; and they gnawed their tongues for pain, 11 and they blasphemed The God of heaven because of their pains and their sores; and they repented not of their works.

12 And the sixth poured out his bowl upon the great river, the [river] Euphrates; and the water thereof was dried up, that the way might by made ready for the kings that [come] from the sun-rising.

17 And the seventh poured out his bowl upon the air; and there came forth a great voice out of the temple, from the throne, saying; "It is done." 18 and there were lightenings, and voices, and thunders; and there was a great earthquake, such as was not since there were men upon the earth, so great an earthquake, so mighty. 19 And the great city was divided into three parts, and the cities of the nations fell and Babylon the great was remembered in the sight of God, to give unto her the cup of the wine of the fierceness of His wrath. 20 And every island fled away, and the mountains were not found. 21 And great

hail, [every stone] about the weight of a tal-
ent, came down out of heaven upon men and
men blasphemed God because of the plague
of the hail for the plague thereof is exceed-
ing great.
17: 1 And there came one of the seven an-
gels that had the seven bowls, and spoke with
me, saying; "Come here, I will show you the
judgment of the great harlot[45] that sits upon
many waters 2 with whom the kings of the
earth committed fornication, and they that
dwell in the earth were made drunken with
the wine of her fornication."
3 And he carried me away in the Spirit into a
wilderness and I saw a woman sitting upon a
scarlet-colored beast, full of names of blas-
phemy, having seven heads and ten horns[46].
4 And the woman was arrayed in purple and
scarlet, and decked with gold and precious
stone and pearls, having in her hand a golden

---

[45] *The false church that existed taught unsuspecting believers their false ways. The same false church directs and guide most other religious groups to follow in her erroneous ways.*

[46] *The false church will control seven specific government with ten nations under them. Two of the governments will be very visible when Christ is about to return.*

cup full of abominations, even the unclean
things of her fornication, 5 and upon her
forehead a name written, MYSTERY,
BABYLON THE GREAT, THE MOTHER OF
THE HARLOTS AND OF THE ABOMINA-
TIONS OF THE EARTH. 6 And I saw the
woman drunken with the blood of the saints,
and with the blood of the martyrs of Jesus.
And when I saw her, I wondered with a great
wonder. 7 And the angel said unto me;
"Wherefore do you wonder? I will tell you
the mystery of the woman, and of the beast
that carry her, which have the seven heads
and the ten horns. 8 The beast that you saw
was, and is not; and is about to come up out
of the abyss, and to go into perdition. And
they that dwell on the earth shall wonder,
whose name have not been written in the
book of life from the foundation of the world,
when they behold the beast, how that he was,
and is not, and shall come. 9 Here is the mind
that have wisdom. The seven heads are seven
mountains, on which the woman sits. 10 and
they are seven kings; the five are fallen, the
one is, the other is not yet come; and when
he comes, he must continue a little while. 11
And the beast that was, and is not, is himself

also an eighth, and is of the seven; and he
goes into perdition. 12 And the ten horns
that you saw are ten kings, who have received
no kingdom as yet; but they receive author-
ity as kings, with the beast, for one hour. 13
These have one mind, and they give their
power and authority unto the beast. 14 These
shall war against the Lamb, and the Lamb
shall overcome them, for He is Lord of lords,
and King of kings; and they that are with Him,
called and chosen and faithful."
19: 11 And I saw the heaven opened; and
behold, a white horse, and He that sat
thereon called Faithful and True; and in righ-
teous He doth judge and make war. 12 And
His eyes a flame of fire, and upon His head
many diadems; and He have a name written
which no one knows but He Himself. 13 And
He [is] arrayed in a garment sprinkled with
blood and His name is called The Word of
God. 14 And the armies which are in heaven
followed Him upon white horses, clothed in
fine linen, white [and] pure. 15 And out of
His mouth proceeds a sharp sword, that with
it He should smite the nations and He shall

rule them with a rod of iron[47] and He treads the winepress of the fierceness of the wrath of God, The Almighty. 16 And He have on His garment and on His thigh a name written, KINGS OF KINGS, AND LORD OF LORDS.

1:7 Behold, He come with the clouds; and every eye shall see Him, and they that pierced Him and all the tribes of the earth shall mourn over Him. Even so, Amen. 8 "I am the Beginning and the End...", said The Lord God, "...who is and who was and who is to come, The Almighty."

7:1 After this I saw four angels standing at the four corners of the earth, holding the four winds of the earth, that no wind should blow on the earth, or on the sea, or upon any tree. 2 And I saw another angel ascend from the sun-rising, having the seal of the living God and he cried with a great voice to the four angels to whom it was given to hurt the earth and the sea,

---

[47] *This is Jesus Christ as prophesied of in Isaiah 11: 1-10*

3 saying, "Hurt not the earth, neither the sea,
nor the trees, till we shall have sealed the ser-
vants of our God on their foreheads."
4 And I heard the number of them that were
sealed, a hundred and forty and four thou-
sand, sealed out of every tribe of the children
of Israel 5 of the tribe of Judah [were] sealed
twelve thousand of the tribe of Reuben twelve
thousand; of the tribe of Gad twelve thou-
sand; 6 of the tribe of Asher twelve thou-
sand; of the tribe of Naphtali twelve thou-
sand; of the tribe of Manasseh twelve thou-
sand; 7 of the tribe of Simeon twelve thou-
sand; of the tribe of Levi twelve thousand; of
the tribe of Issachar twelve thousand; 8 of
the tribe of Zebulun twelve thousand; of the
tribe of Joseph twelve thousand; of the tribe
of Benjamin [were] sealed twelve thousand.

17: 15 And he said unto me, "The waters
which you saw, where the harlot sits, are
peoples, and multitudes, and nations, and
tongues. 16 And the ten horns which thou
saw, and the beast, these shall hate the har-
lot, and shall make her desolate and naked,
and shall eat her flesh, and shall burn her
utterly with fire. 17 For God did put in their

hearts to do His mind, and to come to one mind, and to give their kingdom unto the beast, until the words of God should be accomplished.
18 And the woman whom you saw is the great city, which reign over the kings of the earth."

Destruction Of The False Religion

8 And another, a second angel, followed, saying;

"Fallen, fallen is Babylon the great, that had made all the nations to drink of the wine of the wrath of her fornication."

9 And another angel, a third, followed them, saying with a great voice;

"If any man worship the beast and his image, and receives a mark on his forehead, or upon
his hand, 10 he also shall drink of the wine of the wrath of God, which is prepared unmixed in the cup of His anger; and he shall be tormented with fire and brimstone in the presence of the holy angels, and in the pres-
ence of The Lamb 11 and the smoke of their torment go up forever and ever; and they have no rest day and night, they that worship the beast and his image, and whoso receive the mark of his name"

18:1 After these things I saw another angel
coming down out of heaven, having great
authority; and the earth was lightened with
his glory. 2 And he cried with a mighty voice,
saying;
"Fallen, fallen is Babylon the great, and is
become a habitation of demons, and a hold
of every unclean spirit, and a hold of every
unclean and hateful bird. 3 For by the wine
of the wrath of her fornication all the nations
are fallen; and the kings of the earth com-
mitted fornication with her, and the mer-
chants of the earth waxed rich by the power
of her wantonness."[48]

4 And I heard another voice from heaven,
saying;
"Come forth, my people, out of her, that you
have no fellowship with her sins, and that you
receive not of her plagues 5 for her sins have
reached even unto heaven, and God has re-

---

[48] *Only one nation that possess the ability to affect world commerce, and make men rich because of their trade with her. This is the nation that is Babylon and leads other nations to become an abomination before God.*

membered her iniquities.[49] 6 Render unto her even as she rendered, and double [unto her] the double according to her works in the cup which she mingled, mingle unto her double. 7 How much so ever she glorified herself, and waxed wanton, so much give her of torment and mourning for she said in her heart, I sit a queen, and am no widow, and shall in no wise see mourning.
8 Therefore in one day shall her plagues come, death, and mourning, and famine; and she shall be utterly burned with fire; for strong is The Lord God who judged her."

"9 And the kings of the earth, who committed fornication and lived wantonly with her, shall weep and wail over her, when they look

---

[49] *John 3: 16 All humanity have been living in sin and will continue to pursue this line of existence until Jesus Christ's teachings become their way of life. He shows us how to come out of the sinful path taught by the great false church system: Follow His teachings John 14: 6; following His teachings include keeping the commandments (all of them) John 15:14. This was the emphasis at the start of His ministry, Matthew 5: 17-19. Jesus gave us every instruction to make our path to Him easy: Seek first The Kingdom, Matthew 6:33, employ all effort to strive for perfection, and we will attain perfection, Matthew 5: 48.*

upon the smoke of her burning, 10 stand-
ing afar off for the fear of her torment, say-
ing, 'Woe, woe, the great city, Babylon, the
strong city! for in one hour is your judgment
come.'"

11 And the merchants of the earth weep and
mourn over her, for no man buys their mer-
chandise any more; 12 merchandise of gold,
and silver, and precious stone, and pearls, and
fine linen, and purple, and silk, and scarlet;
and all thyine wood, and every vessel of ivory,
and every vessel made of most precious wood,
and of brass, and iron, and marble; 13 and
cinnamon, and spice, and incense, and oint-
ment, and frankincense, and wine, and oil,
and fine flour, and wheat, and cattle, and
sheep; and [merchandise] of horses and
chariots and slaves; and souls of men. 14 And
the fruits which thy soul lusted after are gone
from you, and all things that were dainty and
sumptuous are perished from you, and shall
find them no more at all. 15 The merchants
of these things, who were made rich by her,
shall stand afar off for the fear of her torment,
weeping and mourning; 16 saying, "Woe,
woe, the great city, she that was arrayed in

fine linen and purple and scarlet, and decked
with gold and precious stone and pearl!"
17 for in an hour so great riches are made
desolate. And every shipmaster, and every
one that sails any wither, and mariners, and
as many as gain their living by sea, stood afar
off, 18 and cried out as they looked upon the
smoke of her burning, saying, What is like
the great city? 19 And they cast dust on their
heads, and cried, weeping and mourning,
saying,
"Woe, woe, the great city, wherein all that had
their ships in the sea were made rich by reason of her costliness! for in one hour is she
made desolate."
20 Rejoice over her, you heaven, and you
saints, and you apostles, and you prophets;
for God have judged your judgment on her.
21 And a strong angel took up a stone as it
were a great millstone and cast it into the sea,
saying, so with a mighty fall shall Babylon,
the great city, be cast down, and shall be
found no more at all. 22 And the voice of
harpers and minstrels and flute-players and
trumpeters shall be heard no more at all in
her; and no craftsman, of whatsoever craft,
shall be found any more at all in you; and

the voice of a mill shall be heard no more at
all in you; 23 and the light of a lamp shall
shine no more at all in you; and the voice of
the bridegroom and of the bride shall be
heard no more at all in you for your mer-
chants were the princes of the earth; for with
your sorcery were all the nations deceived.
24 And in her was found the blood of proph-
ets and of saints, and of all that have been
slain upon the earth.

9 And he said unto me, Write;
"Blessed are they that are bidden to the marriage supper of the Lamb. And he said unto me, these are true words of God."

8 And it was given unto her that she should array herself in fine linen, bright pure for the fine linen is the righteous acts of the saints.[50]

10 And I fell down before his feet to worship him. And he said unto me; "See you do it not I am a fellow-servant with thee and with your

[50] *The bride of Christ, the church of true believers have made herself ready and finally acceptable to meet Christ, Matthew 25:1-13.*

brethren that hold the testimony of Jesus worship God; for the testimony of Jesus is the spirit of prophecy."

20: 4 And I saw thrones, and they sat upon them, and judgment was given unto them and [I saw] the souls of them that had been beheaded for the testimony of Jesus, and for the word of God, and such as worshipped not the beast, neither his image, and received not the mark upon their forehead and upon their hand; and they lived, and reigned with Christ a thousand years. This is the first resurrection. 6 Blessed and holy is he that have part in the first resurrection over these the second death have no power; but they shall be priests of God and of Christ, and shall reign with him a thousand years. 5 The rest of the dead lived not until the thousand years should be finished. **20**:1 And I saw an angel coming down out of heaven, having the key of the abyss and a great chain in his hand. 2 And he laid hold on the dragon, the old serpent, which is the Devil and Satan, and bound him for a thousand years, 3 and cast him into the abyss, and shut, and sealed over him, that he should deceive the nations no more,

until the thousand years should be finished
after this he must be loosed for a little time.

7 And when the thousand years are finished,
Satan shall be loosed out of his prison, 8 and
shall come forth to deceive the nations which
are in the four corners of the earth, Gog and
Magog, to gather them together to the war
the number of whom is as the sand of the
sea. 9 And they went up over the breadth of
the earth, and compassed the camp of the
saints about, and the beloved city and fire
came down out of heaven, and devoured
them.
19:17 And I saw an angel standing in the sun;
and he cried with a loud voice, saying to all
the birds that fly in mid heaven, Come [and]
be gathered together unto the great supper
of God 18 that you may eat the flesh of kings,
and the flesh of captains, and the flesh of
mighty men, and the flesh of horses and of
them that sit thereon, and the flesh of all
men, both free and bond, and small and
great.
19 And I saw the beast, and the kings of the
earth, and their armies, gathered together
to make war against him that sat upon the

horse, and against his army. 20 And the beast was taken, and with him the false prophet that wrought the signs in his sight, wherewith he deceived them that had received the mark of the beast and them that worshipped his image they two were cast alive into the lake of fire that burns with brimstone 21 and the rest were killed with the sword of him that sat upon the horse, [even the sword] which came forth out of His mouth and all the birds were filled with their flesh.

10 And the devil that deceived them was cast into the lake of fire and brimstone, where are also the beast and the false prophet; and they shall be tormented day and night for ever and ever.

11 And I saw a great white throne, and Him that sat upon it, from whose face the earth and the heaven fled away; and there was found no place for them. 12 And I saw the dead, the great and the small, standing before the throne; and books were opened and another book was opened, which is (the book) of life and the dead were judged out of the things which were written in the books,

according to their works. 13 And the sea gave
up the dead that were in it; and death and
Hades gave up the dead that were in them
and they were judged every man according
to their works. 14 and death and Hades were
cast into the lake of fire. This is the second
death, [even] the lake of fire.
15 And if any was not found written in the
book of life, he was cast into the lake of fire.
21: 8 But for the fearful, and unbelieving,
and abominable, and murderers, and fornicators, and sorcerers, and idolaters, and all liars, their part (shall be) in the lake that burns with fire and brimstone; which is the second death.[51]

---

[51] *It is very clear here that The Holy Scripture is a radical departure from what is being taught as mainstream Christian teaching about hell. Hell is a fiery abode able to restrain Satan, his false prophets i.e. strong spiritual beings and hold them forever. However flesh and blood man that is placed into the same abode of spirit prisoners(hell) will suffer the second death.(As if they never existed.) This point makes it clear that there is no existence of living in hell and burning there forever of man. (Please note that man is not made from the same matter as the spirit world. Man can be spiritual, living a life that seeks after spiritual truth but he is not spirit. Man will not be made spirit until he is resurrected or changed at the arrival of the second coming of Jesus Christ.) John 5:24-30, I Cor 15:50-55, I Thes 4:13-18, John 6:38-40, Phili I:6 +:3:20 & 21.*

19:1 After these things I heard as it were a
great voice of a great multitude in heaven,
saying, Hallelujah; Salvation, and glory, and
power, belongs to our God 2 for true and
righteous are His judgments; for He have
judged the great harlot, her that corrupted
the earth with her fornication,[52] and He have
avenged the blood of His servants at her
hand. 3 And a second time they say, Hallelu-
jah. And her smoke goes up forever and ever.
4 And the four and twenty elders and the
four living creatures fell down and wor-
shipped God that sits on the throne, saying,
Amen; Hallelujah.

9 After these things I saw, and behold, a great
multitude,[53] which no man could number,
out of every nation and of [all] tribes and
peoples and tongues, standing before the

---

[52] *True believers who fought to teach God's truth and keep The Truth finally rejoice because the false system that taught lawlessness or the breaking of God's Commandments and laws were OK have now been eradicated, Matthew 7:23. Jesus did warn about this way of living He calls it the Broadway, Matthew 7:13 & 14. All the various teachings through the many worldly denominations will be destroyed and only the way* <u>*Jesus taught and teaches*</u> *will stand.*

throne and before The Lamb, arrayed in
white robes, and palms in their hands; 10 and
they cry with a great voice, saying, "Salvation
unto our God who sits on the throne, and
unto The Lamb." 11 And all the angels were
standing round about the throne, and
[about] the elders and the four living creatures; and they fell before the throne on their
faces, and worshipped God, 12 saying,

"Amen, blessing, and glory, and wisdom, and thanksgiving, and honor, and power, and might, unto our God forever and ever. Amen." I said unto him, "and whence came
these; who are they?" 13 And one of the elders answered, saying unto me, "These that
are arrayed in white robes, 14 And My lord,
you know...." And he said to me, "...These are they that come of the great tribulation, and they washed their robes, and made them white in the blood of the Lamb.

---

[53] *The great multitude are those who heard and followed the teachings of Christ and the ruling 144 thousands who reigned for the millennium. This Includes all whoever lived even before the time of Jesus' first coming. the resurrected dead who lived throughout the ages were given a second chance and changed their ways according to the witness of Jesus Christ. This was after their deeds were measured by the standard of the 'Book Of Life' and they were found worthy.*

15 Therefore they are before the throne of
God; and they serve him day and night in
His temple and He that sits on the throne
shall spread His tabernacle over them. 16
They shall hunger no more, neither thirst
any more; neither shall the sun strike upon
them, nor any heat 17 for The Lamb that is
in the middle of the throne shall be their
Shepherd, and shall guide them unto fountains of waters of life and God shall wipe away
every tear from their eyes."

19: 5 And a voice came forth from the throne,
saying; "Give praise to our God, all you His servants, you that fear Him, the small and the great."
6 And I heard as it were the voice of a great
multitude, and as the voice of many waters, and as the voice of mighty thunders, Saying; "Hallelujah for the Lord our God, The Almighty, reigns.
7 Let us rejoice and be exceeding glad, and
let us give the glory unto Him for the marriage of The Lamb is come, and His wife have made herself ready."

15: 2 And I saw as it were a sea of glass mingled with fire; and them that come off victorious from the beast, and from his image, and from the number of his name, standing by the sea of glass, having harps of God. 3 And they sing the song of Moses the servant of God, and the song of the Lamb, saying,

> Great and marvelous are your works, O Lord God,
> the Almighty; righteous and true are Your ways,
> You, King of the ages.
> 4 Who shall not fear, O Lord,
> and glorify Your Name?
> for You only are holy;
> for all the nations shall come and worship before thee; for Your righteous acts have been made manifest.

21: 9 And there came one of the seven angels who had the seven bowls, who were laden with the seven last plagues; and he spoke with me, saying, "Come here, I will show thee the bride, the wife of the Lamb."
10 And he carried me away in the Spirit to a mountain great and high, and showed me

the holy city Jerusalem[54], coming down out of heaven from God, **21**:1 And I saw a new heaven and a new earth for the first heaven and the first earth are passed away; and the sea is no more. 2 And I saw the holy city, New Jerusalem, coming down out of heaven of God, made ready as a bride adorned for her husband. 11 having the glory of God her light were like unto a stone most precious, as it were a jasper stone, clear as crystal 12 having a wall great and high; having twelve gates, and at the gates twelve angels; and names written thereon, which are of the twelve tribes of the children of Israel

13 on the east were three gates; and on the north three gates; and on the south three gates; and on the west three gates.

14 And the wall of the city had twelve foundations, and on them twelve names of the twelve apostles of the Lamb.

11:1 And there was given me a reed like unto a rod and one said, rise, and measure the temple of God, and the altar, and them that

---

[54] *John 14: 2, God will bring us mansions within His Holy Kingdom for everytrue believer and it will be glorious. It will come down on earth for all who qualify; Matthew 5: 3-10 especially verse five.*

worship therein. 2 And the court which is
without the temple leave without, and measure it not; for it have been given unto the
nations and the holy city shall they tread under foot forty and two months.
15 And he that spoke with me had for a measure a golden reed to measure the city, and
the gates thereof, and the wall thereof.
16 And the city laid foursquare, and the
length thereof is as great as the breadth and
he measured the city with the reed, fifteen
hundred miles the length and the breadth
and the height thereof are equal. 17 And he
measured the wall thereof, a hundred and
forty and four cubits, [according to] the
measure of a man, that is, of an angel.

18 And the building of the wall thereof was
jasper and the city was pure gold, like unto
pure glass. 19 The foundations of the wall of
the city were adorned with all manner of precious stones. The first foundation was jasper;
the second, sapphire; the third, chalcedony;
the fourth, emerald; 20 the fifth, sardonyx;
the sixth, sardius; the seventh, chrysolite; the
eighth, beryl; the ninth, topaz; the tenth,
chrysoprase; the eleventh, jacinth; the twelfth,

amethyst. 21 And the twelve gates were twelve
pearls; each one of the several gates was of
one pearl and the street of the city was pure
gold, as it were transparent glass. 22 And I
saw no temple therein for the Lord God the
Almighty, and the Lamb, are the temple
thereof.
23 And the city had no need of the sun, nei-
ther of the moon, to shine upon it for the
glory of God did lighten it, and the lamp
thereof the Lamb.

22: 1 And he showed me a river of water of
life, bright as crystal, proceeding out of the
throne of God and of the Lamb, 2 in the
middle of the street thereof. And on this side
of the river and on that was the tree of life,
bearing twelve [manner of] fruits, yielding
its fruit every month and the leaves of the
tree were for the healing of the nations. 3
And there shall be no curse any more and
the throne of God and of The Lamb shall be
therein and his servants shall serve him; 4
and they shall see his face; and his name on
their foreheads.
5 And there shall be night no more; and they
need no light of lamp, neither light of sun;

for the Lord God shall give them light and they shall reign forever and ever.

21: 24 And the nations shall walk among the light thereof and the kings of the earth bring their glory into it. 25 And the gates thereof shall in no wise be shut by day (for there shall be no night there) 26 and they shall bring the glory and the honor of the nations into it
21: 3 And I heard a great voice out of the throne saying;
"Behold, the tabernacle of God is with men[55], and he shall dwell with them, and they shall be his peoples, and God himself shall be with them, (and be) their God 4 and he shall wipe away every tear from their eyes; and death shall be no more; neither shall there be mourning, nor crying, nor pain, any more the first things are passed away."

---

[55] *This statement is a stark contrast from what is taught today: The current teaching is that man goes to be with God in heaven. Verse 3 of the 21st chapter shows that man's concept of going to heaven is false. The truth of the matler is that the Kingdom or tabernacle of God, prepared in heaven comes down to be with man not the otherway around.*

5 And He that sits on the throne said, "Be-
hold, I make all things new. And he said;
"Write for these words are faithful and true."
6 And He said unto me;
"They are come to pass. I am the Alpha and
the Omega, the Beginning and the End. I
will give unto him that is thirsty of the foun-
tain of the water of life freely. 7 He that over-
comes shall inherit these things; and I will be
his God, and he shall be my son."

27 and there shall in no wise enter into it
anything unclean, or he that make an abomi-
nation and a lie but only they that are writ-
ten in the Lamb's book of life.

6 And he said unto me; "These words are
faithful and true" and The Lord, The God of
the spirits of the prophets, sent His angels to
show unto his servants the things which must
shortly come to pass. 7 "And behold, I come
quickly. Blessed is he that keeps the words of
the prophecy of this book." 8 And I John am
he that heard and saw these things. And when
I heard and saw, I fell down to worship be-
fore the feet of the angel that showed me
these things. 9 And he said unto me,

"See you do it not, I am a fellow-servant with you and with your brethren the prophets, and with them that keep the words of this book worship God." 10 And he said unto me, "Seal not up the words of the prophecy of this book; for the time is at hand."

11 He that is unrighteous, let him do unrighteousness still and he that is filthy, let him be made filthy still and he that is righteous, let him do righteousness still and he that is holy, let him be made holy still. 12 "Behold, I come quickly; and My reward is with Me, to render to each man according as his work. 13 I am the Alpha and the Omega, the first and the last, the beginning and the end. 14 Blessed are they that wash their robes, that they may have the right [to come] to the tree of life, and may enter in by the gates into the city.

15 Without are the dogs[56], and the sorcerers,

---

[56] *By this time God have made His final judgment, the righteous ones are within God's Kingdom and outside of it is the holding place of the demons and the bodies of evil men being destroyed both humanity and the angels towards whom He finally vents His anger by calling them dogs.*

and the fornicators, and the murderers, and the idolaters, and every one that love and make a lie. 16 I Jesus have sent mine angel to testify unto you these things for the churches. I am the root and the offspring of David, the bright, the morning star.

17 And the Spirit and the bride say, come. And he that hear, let him say, Come. And he that is thirsty, let him come he that will, let him take the water of life freely[57]. 18 I testify unto every man that hear the words of the prophecy of this book, if any man shall add unto them, God shall add unto him the plagues which are written in this book 19 and if any man shall take away from the words of the book of this prophecy, God shall take away his part from the tree of life, and out of the holy city, which are written in this book....."
20 He who testifies these things said, "...Yea I come quickly. Amen"
"Come, Lord Jesus." 21 The grace of the Lord Jesus be with the saints. Amen.

---

[57] *The angel finally takes us to the present time of our lives entreating us to seek Jesus Christ and live according to all His teachings. Adding nothing to the stature and teaching of Christ and taking nothing away! BE WARNED!*

Conclusion

As you close the cover to this book may this be the beginning of you opening the Holy Scriptures as given to us by God that you may live the Christian life as taught and exemplified by Jesus Christ.

The Word of God being very expansive requires so much to be learned. May the process started by Martin Luther continue with you as the Bereans did to understand the accurate teachings of Scriptures; searching The Book daily.

Brethen the end is near let us use our time and energies to fulfill the royal command of Jesus Christ through The Holy Spirit to grow in knowledge as we seek to enter the Kingdom of Heaven.

Much Love to You.

C. Lincoln Humes, Pastor

Notes

Notes

Notes

Notes

Notes

Notes

The Author

C. Lincoln Humes has been a dedicated Christian since 1974 and have stayed strong in his dedication to God and Jesus Christ. He was ordained a Methodist lay minister and preached for many years serving the Lord in Sunday School teaching, youth ministry and a prison ministry. As his spiritual walk matured he realized that there was more to God than just the surface doctrines that were handed down through the traditions of men. He studied the Word of God with a depth motivated by love of God and he gleaned the deep things of God a like that has never been seen before. This is never more evident than in the messages he delivers as a part of his radio broadcast each Sunday. Mr. Humes is reaching many lives with the accurate message of Jesus Christ as he councils and visits individuals who are seeking the ways of the original Church of God formed by the Holy Spirit and Jesus Christ and the early apostles. Personally Mr. Humes grew up in a non-religious family who studied and practiced the occult and at the age of twenty one felt and answered the call of The Lord. He is a former high school arts and crafts teacher, a photo journalist and a movie maker primarily in documentaries. He is also a non-practicing certified Olympic coach in track and field. From time to time he would gather high school age kids teaching them the principle of good sportsmanship. He is most comfortable organizing activities that brings fathers and sons together and organizing back-to-school drive for indigent communities. His love for the under served and their plight is driven by the love generated through The Holy Spirit of God.

His only pledge is that he will never give up until all true believers come to understand and accept the accurate teachings of Jesus Christ and live by them and not just accepting the teachings about Jesus Christ as is pawned off as Chistianity.

Universal Church of God
6718 S. Constance Avenue
Chicago, IL 60649
(773) 324-1144 Phone
(773) 324-2272 Fax
email: hiswayone@yahoo.com

Printed in the United States
35134LVS00001B/58-87

9 781594 082931